Extreme Planets!

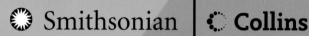 Smithsonian | 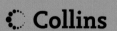 Collins

An Imprint of HarperCollins Publishers

Q&A

Smithsonian Mission Statement

For more than 160 years, the Smithsonian has remained true to its mission, "the increase and diffusion of knowledge." Today the Smithsonian is not only the world's largest provider of museum experiences supported by authoritative scholarship in science, history, and the arts but also an international leader in scientific research and exploration. The Smithsonian offers the world a picture of America, and America a picture of the world.

Special thanks to Dr. James Zimbelman, Planetary Geologist, National Air and Space Museum, Smithsonian Institution, for his invaluable contribution to this book.

This book was created by **jacob packaged goods LLC** (www.jpgglobal.com).
Written by: Mary Kay Carson
Creative: Ellen Jacob, Jeff Chandler, Kirk Cheyfitz, Sarah L. Thomson, Andrea Curley

All photos NASA except: **pages 6–7:** David A. Aguilar/© Harvard-Smithsonian Center for Astrophysics; **page 22:** © Detlev van Ravenswaay/Photo Researchers, Inc.; **pages 38–39:** NASA and G. Bacon (STScI)

2 3 4 5 6 7 8 9 10 ❖ First Edition

Contents

What is a planet? 4

How did the planets form? 6

How do planets move? 8

What planet orbits the sun the fastest? 10

Why is Venus the solar system's
   hottest planet? 12

How fast is Earth moving?
   Why don't you feel it? 14

What's a moon? 16

Why is Mars called the Red Planet? 19

Is there life on Mars?
   Was there ever life on Mars? 20

Are asteroids planets? 22

What is the largest planet? 24

How many moons orbit Jupiter? 27

What are the rings of Saturn? 28

Who discovered Uranus? 30

What's the weather like on Neptune? 33

What about Pluto? 34

Are there more dwarf planets? 36

What's a Kuiper Belt object? 38

Are there planets circling other stars? 41

Are there earthlike planets
   beyond our solar system? 42

Meet the Astronomer 44

Glossary 46

More to See and Read 47

Index 48

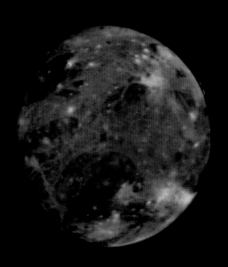

What is a planet?

A **planet** is a large, round space object that circles, or **orbits**, a star.

While all these space objects are round, only Jupiter (top) is a planet. The other four objects are moons of Jupiter.

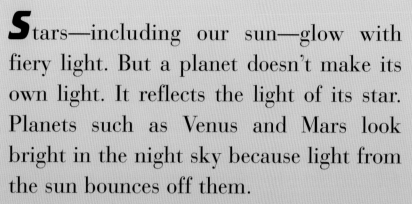

Stars—including our sun—glow with fiery light. But a planet doesn't make its own light. It reflects the light of its star. Planets such as Venus and Mars look bright in the night sky because light from the sun bounces off them.

Planets are alone in their orbits. A planet's orbit—the long oval path it travels around the sun—doesn't cross the orbit of any other planet or any large space object like an **asteroid**.

All planets have the same round shape—that of a **sphere**. Why aren't planets shaped like boxes, tubes, or pyramids? Gravity pulls all objects toward their centers. The heavier something is, the more gravity pulls on it. Planets are so big that gravity has formed them into a shape in which every part is as close to the center as it can get—a sphere.

SMITHSONIAN LINK
Photographs and satellite images of the planets taken during NASA space missions help researchers at the Center for Earth and Planetary Studies in Washington, DC, make new discoveries about our solar system. www.nasm.si.edu/research/ceps/imagery.cfm

How did the planets form?

A sun and its planets are called a **solar system**. Billions of years ago, our solar system was a giant, spinning cloud of dust and gas. As the cloud spun, **gravity** pulled most of the dust and gas into its center, where it created a star. Leftover gas and dust swirled around our new sun and over time became the planets.

Gravity kept the heaviest stuff near the center of the new solar system. As a result, the planets that formed closest to the sun became solid, rocky **terrestrial planets**: Mercury, Venus, Earth, and Mars. Farther from the sun were mostly gases that freeze at low temperatures. The gases froze into ice and formed worlds without any solid land—the **gas giant** planets: Jupiter, Saturn, Uranus, and Neptune.

SMITHSONIAN LINK
If you are in Washington, DC, experience space travel through the Lockheed Martin IMAX theater at the National Air and Space Museum. www.nasm.si.edu/visit/theaters/mall

An artist's rendering of a cocoon of gas and dust that surrounds a star where planets may possibly form.

Our solar system's eight planets are beautiful balls in the black of space. Starting from the top (and closest to the sun): Mercury, Venus, Earth, Mars, Jupiter, Saturn, Uranus, and Neptune.

How do planets move?

The path a planet travels around a star is called its orbit. The time it takes a planet to make one loop around its sun is a **year**. Earth's year is 365 days. Jupiter's trip around the sun takes longer because it's farther away. How long? Jupiter's year is 4,331 Earth days.

Planets also spin like tops. The time it takes a planet to spin around once is a **day**. Bigger planets often spin faster than smaller ones. Earth's day lasts 24 hours. Gas giant Jupiter's day is slightly less than 10 hours. But a planet's spinning speed can change. If a giant space object slams into a planet, it can slow down the planet. Some kind of collision probably caused Venus to spin slowly. Its day lasts 5,832 hours, or 243 Earth days!

> Trace the orbits of the four outer planets—the planets beyond Mars—with your finger. Which has the longest year?

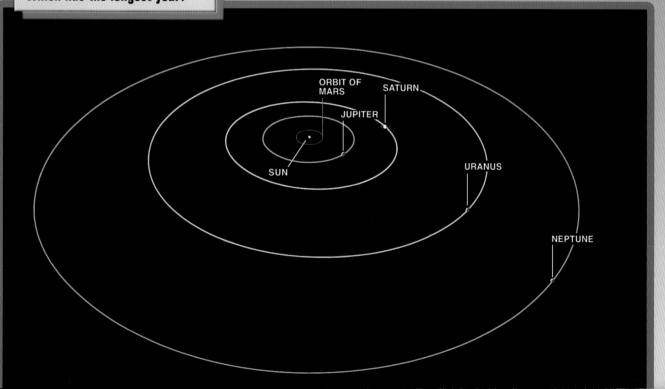

What planet orbits the sun the fastest?

Messenger, a robotic spacecraft with a high-tech protective sunshade, will soon study Mercury.

Mercury is the fastest planet in our solar system, hurtling through space at **104,000** miles per hour.

Mercury's year is short, just about three Earth months, but its day drags on—for 1,407 hours, more than 58 Earth days.

Ten times as much sunlight hits Mercury as Earth. All that glare makes it hard to look at the small planet through a telescope. Being so close to the sun also makes Mercury hard to visit. The sun's strong gravity and intense heat are very hard on spacecraft.

Not long ago, astronomers spotted something unbelievable on Mercury— ice! The frozen water is hidden deep in **craters**. Sunlight never reaches the ice, so it doesn't melt. Mercury is hot only where the sun shines. Nighttime temperatures drop to −279° Fahrenheit because there's no blanket of air on Mercury to hold in the sun's heat. It's Mercury's neighbor Venus that's wrapped in warming air.

Mercury is a gray world covered in craters.

SMITHSONIAN LINK
Learn more about the Messenger mission to Mercury, including when the spacecraft will reach the first planet, at: http://messenger.jhuapl.edu/the_mission/index.html

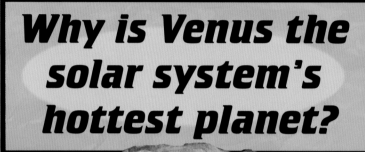

Why is Venus the solar system's hottest planet?

Venus is covered with ancient volcanoes like this one, named Maat Mons.

The air surrounding Venus makes the planet hot enough to melt metal. How can an **atmosphere** heat up a planet? Venus's atmosphere is mostly carbon dioxide. It's the same polluting gas that comes out of car tailpipes and factory smokestacks.

Carbon dioxide in the air traps the sun's rays. It's made Venus so hot that its oceans have boiled away and its land is baked dry. Too much carbon dioxide in Earth's air could overheat us, too. Most scientists think that pollution is warming up our own planet.

Earth and Venus are about the same size. Both are rocky worlds with mountains and valleys. But you wouldn't feel at home on Venus. Even the way time passes there would feel strange. Venus's day lasts longer than its year.

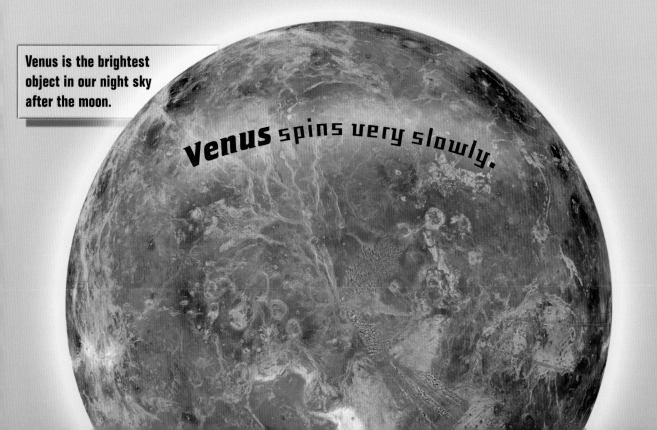

Venus is the brightest object in our night sky after the moon.

Venus spins very slowly.

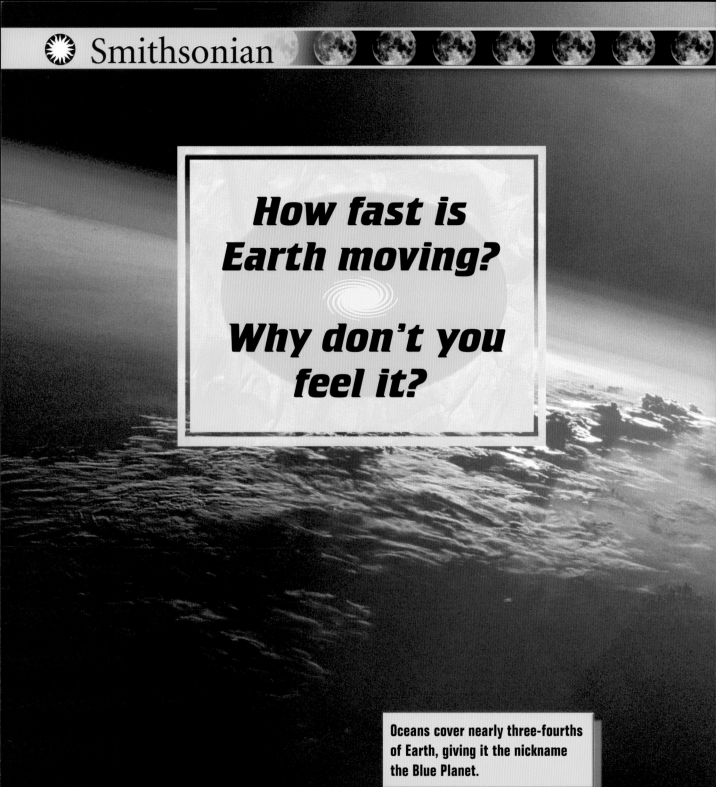

How fast is Earth moving?

Why don't you feel it?

Oceans cover nearly three-fourths of Earth, giving it the nickname the Blue Planet.

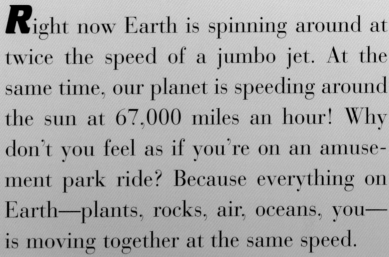

Right now Earth is spinning around at twice the speed of a jumbo jet. At the same time, our planet is speeding around the sun at 67,000 miles an hour! Why don't you feel as if you're on an amusement park ride? Because everything on Earth—plants, rocks, air, oceans, you— is moving together at the same speed.

You can't feel Earth's tilt either. As Earth orbits, part of our planet leans toward the sun and part tilts away from it. It's summer where Earth is tilted toward the sun and winter in the part that's leaning away from it.

Lots of planets have seasons. But Earth's oceans are unique. Liquid water is tough to find on other planets. All life that we know about needs water.

And so far life has been found *nowhere* but here.

SMITHSONIAN LINK
Find out more about what makes our home planet a unique member of the solar system from the online experts at the Harvard-Smithsonian Center for Astrophysics.
www.cfa.harvard.edu/seuforum/opis_tour_earth.htm

What's a moon?

A moon is a natural object that orbits a planet. Scientists think Earth's moon was created as the result of a huge crash. A Mars-sized space object slammed into the young Earth. The blown-up bits of the space object and the pieces it knocked off Earth circled our planet for a while. Over time they clumped together and became our moon. Other planets have moons, too. But not all of them were created the way ours was.

Mars has two moons, named Deimos and Phobos. Both are tiny and shaped a bit like potatoes.

These moons were probably once *space rocks.*

Mars's gravity grabbed the big rocks and trapped them in orbit around the planet.

Our moon is more than a quarter of Earth's size, the biggest moon compared to its planet in our solar system.

Twelve astronauts have walked on Earth's moon. This is a photo of Buzz Aldrin.

No one's found anything **alive** on Mars so far. But scientists haven't finished looking.

The long smilelike slash above is Mars's Valles Marineris, a canyon nearly as long as the United States is wide.

Why is Mars called the Red Planet?

Mars looks like a reddish light in our night sky because the rocks and soil on Mars have lots of iron in them. That iron has rusted and turned everything red. Mars's sky is pink from rusty dust, too.

The Red Planet is a cold desert. Sunny days don't get above freezing. Mars is covered in rocky canyons and mountains, sandy craters, and pebbly plains. There are some amazing sites on Mars. Olympus Mons is a huge, ancient volcano three times taller than Mount Everest!

Like Earth, Mars has four seasons. But Mars's atmosphere is thin, and the air isn't breathable. No trees or animals live on Mars.

Phobos, one of Mars's two tiny moons, is only 17 miles across.

Is there life on Mars?
Was there ever life on Mars?

Spacecraft that land on a planet are called **landers**. Two *Viking* landers set down on Mars in the late 1970s. They scooped up soil and checked it for life—nothing. Life needs water, and Mars didn't seem to have any.

Landers see only a little bit of a planet. **Orbiters** circle above a planet and take photos of all of it. Maps made by Mars orbiters show a desert world with no seas or flowing rivers— but there are dry riverbeds and lake beds. Was Mars once a watery world?

It's the job of wheeled robots, called **rovers**, to find out. Two rovers have discovered proof that water used to cover parts of Mars. Could water still be underground? And could something be living in it? Future spacecraft may tell us.

Both Mars exploration
rovers have cameras,
scientific instruments,
and robotic arms.

SMITHSONIAN LINK
View cool images of Mars and find links
to photos of other planets online at:
www.nasm.si.edu/research/ceps/rpif/mars/mars.html

Rover *Spirit* left a trail of
tire tracks before taking
this picture on Mars.

Are asteroids planets?

Some asteroids pass close by Earth on their way around the sun.

Large space rocks are called asteroids. The moon's many craters were made by asteroids, as well as **comets**, crashing into its surface. Rocks from space have hit Earth, too. An asteroid plowed into our planet 65 million years ago. It blasted so much dust into the air that sunlight couldn't shine through. This made Earth dark and cold and may have helped kill off the dinosaurs.

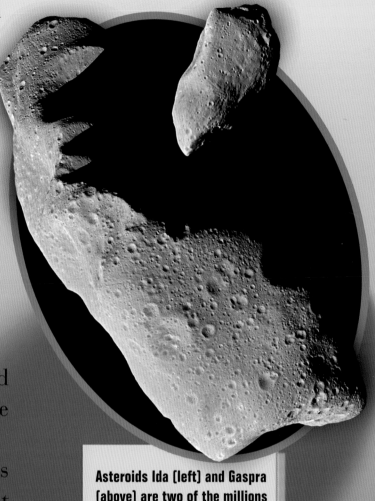

Asteroids often circle stars the same way planets do. Most of our solar system's asteroids orbit the sun in a ring between Mars and Jupiter called the asteroid belt. But most asteroids are too small to be forced into spheres by gravity, so they are not planets.

The biggest asteroid in our solar system, Ceres, is in a

Asteroids Ida (left) and Gaspra (above) are two of the millions of orbiting members of the asteroid belt.

special class. It's more than 500 miles wide, big enough that gravity has made it round. But it orbits in the same path with many other asteroids, so it is not a planet. It's called a **dwarf planet**.

What is the largest planet?

Jupiter is the biggest planet in our solar system. All the other seven planets put together wouldn't weigh half as much as Jupiter.

You could fit 1,300 Earths inside it.

The bigger something is, the more gravity it has. Spacecraft can use Jupiter's gravity to boost their speed. Jupiter pulls at a spacecraft, speeding it up as it falls toward the planet. But before it gets too close, the spacecraft swerves. It's flung away at top speed!

Spacecraft can't land on Jupiter. There is no land on gas giant planets. Jupiter's colored stripes and swirls are icy clouds.

Its atmosphere is so thick, it crushes metal like a paper cup.

The *Galileo* spacecraft dropped a **probe** into Jupiter's atmosphere. It studied the weather for 58 minutes before crumpling.

Jupiter's Great Red Spot (below) is a giant storm as wide as two Earths.

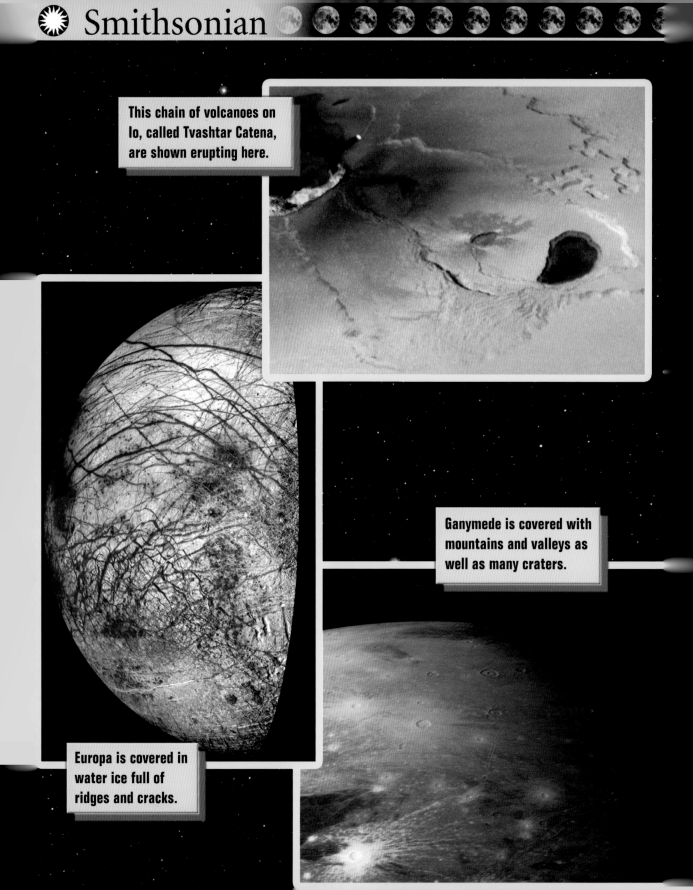

This chain of volcanoes on Io, called Tvashtar Catena, are shown erupting here.

Ganymede is covered with mountains and valleys as well as many craters.

Europa is covered in water ice full of ridges and cracks.

How many moons orbit Jupiter?

Sixty-three moons orbit Jupiter. Many are like rocky terrestrial planets. The famous Italian astronomer Galileo Galilei discovered Jupiter's four biggest moons in 1610. Galileo spotted them using a new telescope he'd made. Someone else named them Ganymede, Io, Callisto, and Europa. But we still call them the Galilean moons.

All four of the Galilean moons are amazing worlds. Io has more volcanoes than any other place in the solar system. Ganymede is the largest moon in the solar system. Europa may have an ocean under its frozen surface. And Callisto is covered in craters. Scientists think that there could be life on Jupiter's large moons. What kind of life? Maybe something like the tube worms and spider crabs that live on Earth's deepest ocean floors.

Callisto is the solar system's most heavily cratered world and Jupiter's darkest large moon.

SMITHSONIAN LINK
Go here to see satellite images of Jupiter and its many moons:
www.nasm.si.edu/research/ceps/rpif/jupiter/jupiter.html

Saturn is the easiest planet to recognize because of its thick belt of rings. Saturn's rings are made of bits of ice and rock. Some chunks are as big as buses. Others are smaller than grains of sand. The stuff of Saturn's rings probably came from asteroids, comets, and moons that broke apart.

More than rings circle Saturn. The second-largest planet has many moons, too—at least 56. Saturn's moon Titan is the second largest in the solar system.

You cannot see Titan from Earth without a telescope. And you also need a telescope to see Saturn's rings. But you can spy Saturn in the night sky.

It's the most *distant planet* that can be seen with the naked eye.

SMITHSONIAN LINK
Visit this link to view images of Titan taken during the Cassini missions.
http://saturn.jpl.nasa.gov/multimedia/images/index.cfm

What are the rings of Saturn?

Saturn and all its rings would just fit between the Earth and its moon.

Who discovered Uranus?

Uranus is a gas giant, so it has no continents, mountains, or even rocks.

People on Earth have watched Mercury, Venus, Mars, Jupiter, and Saturn in the night sky for thousands of years. But in 1781 William Herschel looked through his telescope and became the first person to see a new planet. It was named Uranus.

Two hundred and five years went by before a spacecraft, *Voyager 2*, visited the seventh planet. It found a cold, dark, strange place. If you think of the sunlight that hits Earth as equal to four dollars, only a penny's worth of sunlight reaches Uranus.

Uranus spins lying on its side, like a pearl on a string. Spinning on its side means that one end of Uranus gets sunlight for more than 20 years straight. Meanwhile, the other end is totally dark. Imagine not having seen the sun yet in your lifetime!

Voyager 2 was the only spacecraft to ever visit Uranus. It also flew past Jupiter, Saturn, and Neptune.

SMITHSONIAN LINK
See and read about William Herschel's revolutionary 20-foot reflector telescope online at:
www.nasm.si.edu/exhibitions/gal111/universe/etu_a_herschel.htm

A layer of methane, a natural gas, gives Neptune its deep blue color.

What's the weather like on Neptune?

Neptune is a cold, dark, stormy world. Winds whip at 1,200 miles per hour. Temperatures are always hundreds of degrees below zero. A huge storm, called the Great Dark Spot, swirls on Neptune. It's as big as Earth. Neptune's winds are so strong that they move this monster storm around the planet.

Neptune is far from the sun. How far? Think of days on a calendar. If Earth is about one day from the sun, Saturn is nine days away. And Neptune is a whole month from the sun! It takes Neptune 165 years to complete its orbit. Neptune hasn't finished a single orbit since it was discovered in 1846.

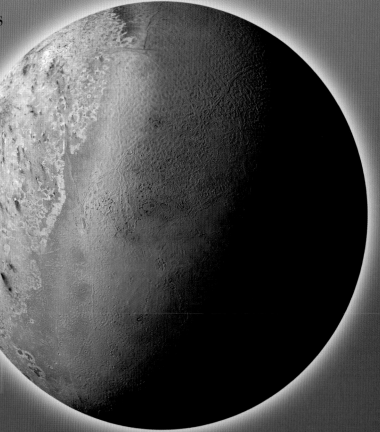

The largest of Neptune's 13 moons is Triton, the coldest known place in the solar system.

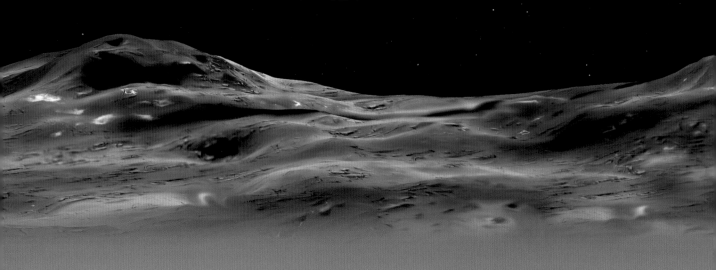

What about Pluto?

For a long time, tiny Pluto was called the ninth planet—the smallest, darkest, and coldest of the worlds orbiting our sun. But in 2006, seventy-six years after it was discovered, astronomers decided that Pluto is not a planet after all.

For one thing, Pluto's orbit crosses Neptune's. For another, astronomers discovered more space objects orbiting in the darkness near Pluto. Since Pluto isn't alone in its orbit, it can't be a planet. However, it *is* big enough to be round.

An artist's view of Pluto (left) and its largest moon, Charon (right), seen from the surface of Hydra or Nix, Pluto's other two small moons.

Like Ceres, Pluto is a dwarf planet.

Dwarf planets aren't really planets, even though the word "planet" is part of their name. Planets and dwarf planets are two separate groups. There are only eight planets orbiting the sun, but we're not sure yet how many dwarf planets there may be.

SMITHSONIAN LINK
Check out these Smithsonian images of Pluto and its moon Charon. Charon is almost half the size of Pluto.
www.nasm.si.edu/research/ceps/etp/pluto/pluto_img.html

Are there more dwarf planets?

One dwarf planet orbiting out beyond Neptune was initially identified as 2003 UB313 by the International Astronomical Union, or IAU. In 2006 the IAU, the scientific group that names asteroids, stars, and other space objects, changed the name of 2003 UB313 to Eris.

The discoverers of Eris say it's as big as Pluto, and maybe bigger. It has at least one moon.

It's a dark, icy, and very far-away world, three times as far from the sun as Pluto. A single orbit takes about 560 Earth years!

For a while it seemed that Eris might be called the tenth planet (after Pluto, which was the ninth for a long time). But in 2006 astronomers decided that there are only eight planets in our solar system.

Eris, like Pluto and Ceres, is a dwarf planet. And these three aren't the only ones.

These three photographs of Eris, with the dwarf planet circled, were taken through a powerful telescope.

An artist's view of Eris and the faintly shining faraway sun.

What's a Kuiper Belt object?

It's always dark at the edges of the solar system. But it's not empty. There are thousands—maybe many thousands—of ice chunks that circle the sun in a wide band. This ring of icy rocks is called the **Kuiper Belt**. The orbiting hunks of ice are called Kuiper Belt objects, or KBOs.

The Kuiper Belt begins past Neptune—not Pluto. Pluto is inside the Kuiper Belt. This means that Pluto is a KBO as well as a dwarf planet. Eris is also a big KBO. We don't know yet how many KBOs are big enough and round enough to be called dwarf planets.

Maybe **dozens**— maybe **hundreds!**

Kuiper Belt objects are leftovers from when the solar system formed.

An artist's view of Sedna, a large, reddish KBO with a tiny moon.

The Orion Nebula is full of young stars surrounded by swirling dust that could become planet-filled solar systems.

Are there planets circling other stars?

Planets beyond our solar system are called **extrasolar planets**. But you can't see them with telescopes. They are lost in the glare of their stars. So how do astronomers find extrasolar planets without seeing them?

A planet's gravity pulls on the star it circles. As a star is tugged toward its orbiting planet, it sways back and forth a bit. The swaying tells astronomers that there's a planet circling a star: the bigger the movement back and forth, the bigger the planet.

Astronomers have found more than 183 extrasolar planets already. So far the worlds we've found beyond our solar system are mostly gas giants, but some have solid land. Smaller terrestrial planets are out there too.

An artist's idea of what one newly found extrasolar planet might look like.

Are there earthlike planets beyond our solar system?

It's hard to spot the tiny swaying that the gravity of an Earth-sized world causes in the star it orbits. But scientists may soon be able to track down small terrestrial planets through the PlanetQuest program. PlanetQuest will use both telescopes and spacecraft to search for earthlike planets. Scientists are working on giant telescopes that can actually see big extrasolar planets—not just their stars wobbling. And a spacecraft called Terrestrial Planet Finder may eventually be developed to send back the first photographs of terrestrial extrasolar planets.

Why hunt for small terrestrial planets? Scientists think that small rocky worlds orbiting ordinary stars might have air—and water. Any place with water is a good place to look for life. Perhaps life is plentiful out in space. Just as planets are.

Terrestrial Planet Finder will use visible light and infrared observatories to discover possible life-supporting planets.

SMITHSONIAN LINK
Visit "What's New in Planetary Exploration" at the National Air and Space Museum online to learn about the most current news in our solar system!
www.nasm.si.edu/research/ceps/etp/wn/etpwn.html

An artist's view of a newly found terrestrial planet, about the size of 13 Earths, with its moon.

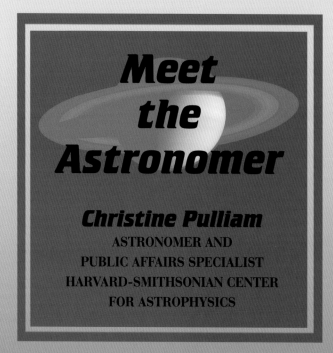

Meet the Astronomer

Christine Pulliam

ASTRONOMER AND
PUBLIC AFFAIRS SPECIALIST
HARVARD-SMITHSONIAN CENTER
FOR ASTROPHYSICS

Christine Pulliam has helped look for extrasolar planets and now teaches people about the wonderful discoveries being made about our universe every day.

Why did you become a scientist?

I have always been interested in space for as long as I can remember. I got my first telescope when I was 13, and I've been hooked on the sky ever since!

What is the most important question you are trying to answer with your research?

I look for planets around other stars. That will answer a very important question: Are we alone? Is Earth the only place with life?

When you were growing up, did you want to be a scientist or something else?

I wanted to be a paleontologist and study dinosaurs. Then I thought I wanted to be an astronaut, but I get airsick and I was afraid that I would get spacesick! So I decided to keep my feet on the ground and study space by becoming an astronomer.

Did you read books or watch TV shows about outer space?

I was a big fan of *Star Trek*. I also read lots of science fiction.

If you couldn't be a scientist, what would you want to be?

If I weren't an astronomer, I think I would like to be a spy. It would be thrilling to sneak into places you're not supposed to go and learn secret information.

What was the most exciting thing that happened to you in your job?

Watching a broken-apart comet hit the planet Jupiter in 1994.

Do you work by yourself or with other people?

I work with other people all the time. Science is a collaborative effort, which means that a lot of people work on the same question to try to find the right answer. No one can know everything, so with a lot of people who each know some things, eventually we hope to get it all figured out.

If I want to be a scientist when I grow up, what should I study now?

Whichever science you find most interesting. Math classes are a good idea. Finally, be sure to learn how to write well because you have to be able to tell people about the research that you want to do and the neat discoveries that you have made.

Do you think that there is life in outer space? Do you think we'll ever meet intelligent alien life?

Yes, I think that there is life in outer space. Intelligent life is a tougher question. I don't believe any aliens have visited Earth yet, and you would think that someone out there would have the technology to come here. But I think the universe would be a very lonely place if there weren't intelligent aliens somewhere. So I think that intelligent alien life is out there, and I hope we will meet it someday.

Glossary

asteroid—A rocky space object that orbits the sun.

astronomer—A scientist who studies space objects.

atmosphere—The air or gases that surround a space object.

comet—A space object made of dust, frozen water, and gases that orbits the sun.

crater—A bowl-shaped hole made by an asteroid or comet crashing into another space object.

day—The time it takes a planet to spin around once.

dwarf planet—A round space object that orbits a star and whose orbit crosses that of another planet or other large space object.

extrasolar planet—A planet outside of our solar system.

gas giant—A large planet of gas with no land.

gravity—The force that pulls objects toward each other.

Kuiper Belt—A ring of orbiting icy chunks called Kuiper Belt objects (KBOs) at the edge of the our solar system.

lander—A spacecraft that sets down on a space object's surface.

moon—A natural space object that orbits a planet, asteroid, or other space object larger than itself.

orbit—The path followed by one space object as it travels around another space object.

orbiter—A spacecraft that orbits a space object.

planet—A large, round space object that orbits a star and whose orbit does not cross that of any other planet or large space object, such as an asteroid.

probe—A robotic spacecraft with no crew.

rover—A robot for exploring the surface of a space object.

solar system—A star and everything that orbits it.

sphere—A ball-shaped object.

terrestrial planet—A rocky, solid planet.

year—The time it takes a planet to make one trip, or orbit, around its sun.

More to See and Read

Go to a Planetarium

Many cities have planetariums. Find one by looking for "planetarium" in the phone book. You can also search for a nearby planetarium at www.museumsusa.org.

Websites

There are links to many wonderful web pages in this book. But the web is constantly growing and changing, so we cannot guarantee that the sites we recommend will be available. If the site you want is no longer there, you can always find your way to plenty of information about the planets through the main Smithsonian website: www.si.edu.

This NASA site has nearly everything you'd ever want to know about the solar system, including the latest discoveries, mission news, and planetary facts for kids. www.solarsystem.nasa.gov

Windows to the Universe space science website is written at three reading levels and in English and Spanish. www.windows.ucar.edu

StarChild website has information on the planets for young astronomers at two reading levels. http://starchild.gsfc.nasa.gov

NASA's Space Place website has information, games, projects, and fun activities about the planets. http://spaceplace.jpl.nasa.gov

Keep track of the search for extrasolar planets at NASA's PlanetQuest website. Also check out "Four Ways to Find a Planet" and take an "Alien Safari." http://planetquest.jpl.nasa.gov

Suggested Reading

The Near Planets by Robin Kerrod. Learn about the similarities and differences among the four planets closest to the sun: Mercury, Venus, Earth, and Mars.

The Far Planets by Robin Kerrod. Jupiter, Saturn, Uranus, and Neptune are the focus of this book.

Exploring Space with an Astronaut by Patricia J. Murphy. Murphy describes the work of astronaut scientists who travel on the space shuttle to study outer space and do onboard experiments.

Eyewitness Mars by Stuart Murray. This wonderfully illustrated guide to the Red Planet is full of facts about Earth's closest neighbor.

The Mystery of Life on Other Planets by Chris Oxlade. This book examines the question of life on other planets and how the space program is looking for possible extraterrestrial life.

Exploring Our Solar System by Sally Ride and Tam O'Shaughnessy. Astronaut Ride and educator O'Shaughnessy offer a lively introduction to our solar system.

Our Solar System by Seymour Simon. Gives young readers a detailed look at all eight planets and more.

Index

Aldrin, Buzz, 17
asteroid, 5, 22–23, 28, 36
asteroid belt, 23
astronaut, 17
astronomer, 11, 27, 34, 36, 41
atmosphere, 13, 19, 24

Callisto, 27
carbon dioxide, 13
Ceres, 23, 35, 36
Charon, 35
cloud, 6, 24
comet, 23, 28
crater, 11, 19, 23, 26, 27

day, 9, 11, 13, 33
Deimos, 16
dinosaurs, 23
dust, 6, 7, 19, 23, 40
dwarf planet, 23, 35, 36, 38

Earth (the Blue Planet), 6, 8, 11,
    31, 33
  and asteroids, 23
  and carbon dioxide, 13
  day, 9, 11
  liquid water, 15
  orbit of, 9, 14–15
  seasons of, 15, 19
  size of, 13, 24, 33
Earth's moon, 13, 16, 17
  craters on, 23
  formation of, 16
Eris (2003 UB313), 36, 37, 38
Europa, 26, 27

Galilei, Galileo, 27
Galileo, 24
Ganymede, 26, 27
Gaspra, 23
gravity, 5, 6, 11, 16, 23, 24, 41, 42

Herschel, William, 31
Hydra, 35

ice, 6, 11, 24, 26, 27, 28, 36, 38
Ida, 23
Io, 26, 27

Jupiter, 6, 8, 9, 23, 24, 25, 31
  moons of, 4, 26–27

Kuiper Belt, 38
Kuiper Belt objects (KBOs), 38, 39

lander, 20
life, 15, 42
light, 5, 11, 19, 31

Mars (the Red Planet), 5, 6, 8, 18,
    19, 21, 23, 31
  moons of, 16
  search for life on, 18, 19–20
Mercury, 6, 8, 10, 11, 31
Messenger, 10
methane, 32
moon, 16, 36

Neptune, 6, 8, 31, 32–33, 34, 38
Nix, 35

ocean, 13, 14, 15, 27
Olympus Mons, 19
orbit, 4, 5, 9, 16, 23, 34, 35, 36,
    38, 41, 42
orbiter, 20
Orion Nebula, 40

Phobos, 16, 19
planet, 4–5, 9
  extrasolar, 41, 42
  formation of, 6
  gas giant, 6, 24, 30, 41
  movement of, 8, 9, 41
  terrestrial, 6, 41
PlanetQuest, 42
Pluto, 34–35, 36, 38
probe, 24

robot, 20
rock, 28, 30, 38
rover, 20, 21

Saturn, 6, 8, 28, 29, 31, 33
  rings of, 28, 29
seasons, 15
Sedna, 39
solar system, 8, 36, 38, 39, 40, 41,
    42
  formation of, 6
spacecraft, 10, 11, 20, 24, 31, 42
space rocks, 16, 23
sphere, 5, 23
Spirit, 21
star, 4, 5, 6, 7, 9, 23, 36, 40, 41,
    42
sun, 5, 6, 8, 9, 22, 23, 35, 36, 37,
    38

telescope, 11, 27, 28, 29, 31, 37,
    41, 42
Terrestrial Planet Finder, 42
Triton, 33
Tvashtar Catena, 26

Uranus, 6, 8, 30, 31

Valles Marineris, 18
Venus, 5, 6, 8, 9, 11, 12–13, 31
Viking, 20
volcano, 12, 19, 26, 27
Voyager 2, 31

water, 11, 15, 20, 26, 27, 42
weather, 24, 33

year, 9, 11, 13, 31, 33, 36